YELLOW ELEPHANT
A BRIGHT BESTIARY

Poems by Julie Larios

Paintings by Julie Paschkis

HARCOURT, INC. ORLANDO AUSTIN NEW YORK SAN DIEGO TORONTO LONDON

Library of Congress
Cataloging-in-Publication Data
Larios, Julie Hofstrand, 1949–
Yellow elephant/Julie Larios;
illustrated by Julie Paschkis.
p. cm.
1. Animals—Juvenile poetry.
2. Colors—Juvenile poetry.
3. Children's poetry, American.
I. Paschkis, Julie. II. Title.
PS3562.A7233Y45 2006
811'.54—dc22 2004025163
ISBN-13: 978-0152-05422-9
ISBN-10: 0-15-205422-7

First edition
H G F E D C B A

Manufactured in China

The illustrations in this book were done in
gouache on Arches paper.

The display and text type were set in
Worcester Round.

Color separations by Colourscan Co. Pte. Ltd.,
Singapore

Manufactured by South China Printing
Company, Ltd., China

This book was printed on totally chlorine-free
Stora Enso Matte paper.

Production supervision by Ginger Boyer

Designed by Linda Lockowitz

For Fernando
—J. L.

For Stephen Iino
—J. P.

CONTENTS

GREEN FROG

One thing for sure
about a green frog
on a green lily pad
on a green day
in spring:
One hop
and her green
is gone.
See how she swims,
blue frog now
under blue water.

RED DONKEY

Red clay road.
Red donkey braying.
He has a red temper.
He's probably saying,
This load is too heavy.
I'm hungry.
My feet hurt!
I'm tired!
I'm hot!
It's
not
fair!
Red donkey sits down.
Someone shouts, "Come!"
But he won't come.
Red donkey tantrum.

WHITE OWL

Who?
asks the white owl,
all eyes.
Who?
This is his riddle.
In the world's white weather,
who has white feathers?
Who flies over white ice?
Who?
And over white snow?
Who flies while the white wind blows?

ORANGE GIRAFFE

Orange sun rising
over the savanna—
can you see the orange water
of the Juba River?
Can you hear the hyena's
high orange laugh?
Look!
On the riverbank,
an orange giraffe.

YELLOW ELEPHANT

Yellow elephant
in the jungle sun,
in the day's yellow heat,
trumpeting her song
and galumphing along.
Oh,
I think no other animal can
(I know a mosquito can't)
glow in the jungle sun
like a wild-eared
yellow elephant.

PURPLE PUPPY

Purple ball for the puppy.
He's feeling pretty nippy.
Needs to run, maybe.
Chases purple birds
and furry squirrels—
he's zigging, they're zagging.
Puppy tail wags.
Now he drinks cool water
with his purple tongue
slurping.

PINK KITTY

Pink collar.
Pink bell.
Pink pillow.
Pink bowl.
And a pink yawn at dawn.
Outside, the city—hot and hazy.
Inside, cool kitty
feeling pink and lazy.

BLACK FISH

Now all silver quiver.
Now all dark flash.
She's all water and wonder,
this black fish.

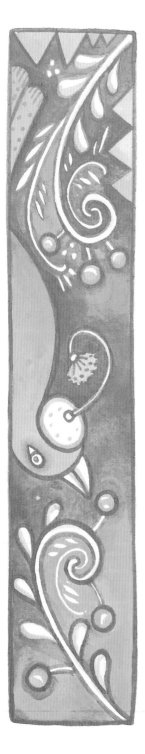

GOLD FINCH

Clinging to a prickly thistle,
the gold finch flutters, whistles,
then flies away.
Some say
his song is only as long
as his tail feathers,
three gold notes
that float.

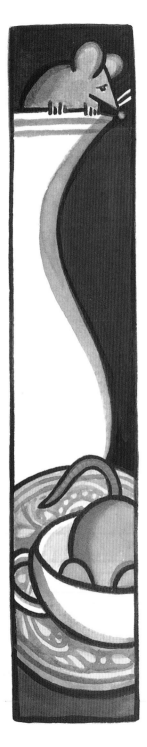

BROWN MOUSE

Little brown clown,
looking for crumbs,
comes sneaking, sniffing, skittering
all around—sounds
like she's jitterbugging
on tinfoil, sharp toenails
clicking and clacking
through the house.
She's in a hurry,
that's for sure,
this brown mouse.

SILVER GULL

Silver gull
on a cedar pole
in the salt water
sees a silver heron
with his beady eyes on the tide.
Summer fog
hides the birds, hides the boulders,
hides the silver beach logs.

TURQUOISE LIZARD

Thunder rolls
across the desert,
quieting the buzz
of the cicadas.
One worried lizard
zips quickly
under a rock.
When raindrops fall,
the small lizard,
turquoise tail curled,
stays bright and dry
in the wet world.

BLUE TURTLE

Slow
in the blue shade
of a blue-leafed garden.
Slow
in the blue gloam.
Hard-shelled and unsudden,
the blue turtle in cool dirt,
heading home.

GRAY GOOSE

Gray mama goose
in a tizzy,
honk-honk-honking herself dizzy,
can't find her gosling,
she's honking and running,
webbed feet slapping,
all wild waddle,
her feathers a muddle,
splashing through puddles,
wings flapping. . . .

Ah,
there's her gold baby,
all fuzz,
napping.

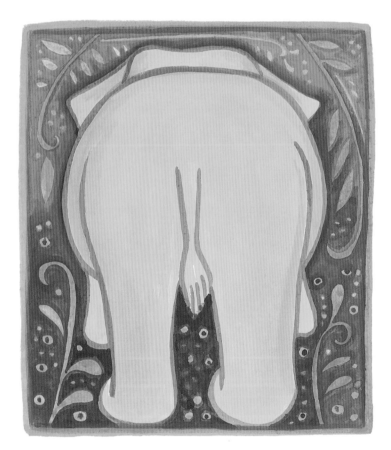